¡BÉISBOL!

LATINO BASEBALL PIONEERS AND LEGENDS

by Jonah Winter

introduction by Bruce Markusen Rodríguez

Lee & Low Books Inc.
New York

For Sally — J.W.

Text and Illustrations copyright © 2001 by Jonah Winter
Introduction copyright © 2001 by Lee & Low Books Inc.

LEE & LOW BOOKS Inc., 95 Madison Avenue, New York, NY 10016
leeandlow.com

The publisher would like to thank Milton H. Jamail, baseball consultant and author of *Full Count: Inside Cuban Baseball,* for his help with the preparation of this book.

Manufactured in China by South China Printing Co.

Book design by Tania Garcia
Book production by The Kids at Our House

The text is set in Bembo
The illustrations are rendered in acrylic

(HC) 10 9 8 7 6 5 4 3 2
(PB) 10 9 8 7 6 5 4 3 2 1
First Edition

Library of Congress Cataloging-in-Publication Data
Winter, Jonah.
    ¡Béisbol! Latino baseball pioneers and legends / Jonah Winter ; introduction by Bruce Markusen Rodríguez.— 1st ed.
        p.   cm.
    ISBN 1-58430-012-4 (hardcover)   ISBN 1-58430-234-8 (paperback)
    1. Baseball players—Latin America—Biography—Juvenile literature.
2. Baseball players—United States—Biography—Juvenile literature.
[1. Baseball players. 2. Latin Americans—Biography. 3. Hispanic Americans—Biography.] I. Title.
GV865.A1 W555 2001
796.357'092'368—dc21
[B]   00-035419

I became a baseball fan because of my father, who bought me baseball books and took me to games at Yankee Stadium. I became a fan of Latino baseball for different reasons, mostly because of my mother's heritage. She was Puerto Rican, making me a proud Latin American.

Not surprisingly, Roberto Clemente, the great Puerto Rican player, was one of my heroes. Sadly, he died in a plane crash in 1972, when I was only seven years old. I started to read books about Clemente and learned that he, like most Latino players before him, had to overcome numerous obstacles. Many Latin American players did not speak English well and were considered unintelligent simply because they could not express their thoughts clearly. Latino players who had dark skin faced additional problems. Like African Americans, they were often called racist names and were treated as second-class citizens. Because of this, some of the greatest Latino players never played in the major leagues. Instead, they played in the Negro Leagues in the United States or the winter leagues in Latin America.

As we enter a new century of baseball, Latin American players dominate the game like never before. Yet the accomplishments of today's Latino stars would not have been possible without the groundbreaking achievements of the 14 Latino trailblazers profiled in this book, all of whom played some part of their careers between 1900 and the 1960s. They have helped make baseball, now fully integrated with Latin American and African American players, a better game.

Bruce Markusen Rodríguez

★ ★ José Méndez ★ ★

YEARS PLAYED: 1908 – 1927

MAIN TEAMS: U.S.: Cuban Stars, Kansas City Monarchs
CUBA: Almendares

POSITIONS: Pitcher, Shortstop, Second Baseman,
Third Baseman, Outfielder, Manager

HEIGHT: 5'8"

WEIGHT: 155 lbs.

BORN: March 19, 1887, Cárdenas, Matanzas, Cuba

DIED: October 31, 1928, Havana, Cuba

José de la Caridad Méndez was the first Latino baseball legend ever. In his homeland of Cuba, they called him "El Diamante Negro," The Black Diamond.

Barred from the major leagues because of his dark skin, The Black Diamond nonetheless sparkled in Cuban baseball and the Negro Leagues in the United States. During the first quarter of the 20th century, there was no better pitcher. That was the opinion of many, including the great major league manager John McGraw. Although McGraw did not hire Méndez to pitch on his all-white team, he did secretly hire the Cuban pitcher to coach his own pitchers. That's what it was like for dark-skinned players in the early 1900s.

What made Méndez so great? Although he was small for a pitcher, he had very strong arms and shoulders. Supposedly, this strength came from chopping sugar cane as a young man in Cuba. Wherever his strength came from, it allowed Méndez to throw deadly, bone-breaking fastballs. His long fingers allowed him to put extra spin on the ball. And his smooth delivery and quick release allowed him to catch batters totally off guard.

All this added up to an incredible .747 lifetime winning percentage in Cuba. And it was in Cuba that El Diamante Negro regularly beat the greatest major league pitchers in exhibition games. Sometimes, when Méndez walked into restaurants in Cuba, people stood up and clapped.

José Méndez

Dolf Luque

YEARS PLAYED: 1912–1946

MAIN TEAMS: U.S.: Cincinnati Reds, New York Giants
   CUBA: Almendares

POSITION: Pitcher

HEIGHT: 5'7"

WEIGHT: 160 lbs.

BORN: August 4, 1890, Havana, Cuba

DIED: July 3, 1957, Havana, Cuba

Adolfo "Dolf" Luque was the first Latin American superstar in the major leagues. Like José Méndez, he was a great Cuban pitcher. But because Luque was light skinned, he was able to enjoy a 20-year career in the U.S. major leagues. "The Pride of Havana," as Luque was called in Cuba, knew this racism wasn't fair. One time, after appearing in a Cuban parade held in his honor, Luque saw Méndez sitting on a bench. He walked over and told Méndez, "This parade should be for you. You're the better pitcher."

Nonetheless, Luque was an excellent player. His lifetime earned run average (ERA) was 3.24. That's better than many Hall of Fame pitchers. Over his major league career, Luque won 194 games, and he was the first Latino to pitch in a World Series, winning both games he pitched. In 1923, Luque led the National League with an amazing 27 wins, a .773 winning percentage, and a 1.93 ERA. But that tells only part of the story. Playing winter baseball in Cuba, he had a lifetime 106–59 win-loss record. Luque pitched for an incredible 35 years, retiring at age 55.

Newspaper writers in the United States said Luque had a bad temper because once he got angry and accidentally hit the famous Casey Stengel with a baseball bat. Maybe that's why Dolf Luque has not yet been elected to the National Baseball Hall of Fame. There could be no other reason.

Dolf Luque

Cristóbal Torriente

YEARS PLAYED: 1913–1928

MAIN TEAMS: U.S.: Cuban Stars, Chicago American Giants CUBA: Almendares

POSITION: Center Fielder

HEIGHT: 5'9"

WEIGHT: 190 lbs.

BORN: 1895, Cuba

DIED: 1938, New York, New York

Cristóbal Torriente was called the "Cuban Babe Ruth." Yet when Babe Ruth played against Torriente's team in Cuba, Torriente got more hits and more home runs than the mighty Ruth. Ruth hit .348 and got two homers. Torriente hit .378 and got three home runs!

Torriente's lifetime batting average against major league pitchers in exhibition games was .311. In Cuba, he still holds the third highest lifetime batting average ever: .351. Torriente got his hits any way he could, frequently swinging at some of the worst balls the pitchers tossed. And often, the broad-shouldered slugger knocked his hits out of the park. This alone would have been enough to guarantee him the status of legend, but Torriente also ran with lightning speed. Not only that, old-timers still rank Torriente as one of the two or three best outfielders in Negro League history. His lifetime Negro League batting average was .327. A manager in the Negro Leagues once said of Torriente, "There walks a ball club."

Cristóbal Torriente was a fierce competitor, and he loved the spotlight, too. He often wore bracelets on his wrists and a red bandanna around his neck. Right before he was about to hit a home run, Torriente would jangle his bracelets.

Cristóbal Torriente

★ ★ Martín Dihigo ★ ★

YEARS PLAYED: 1923–1947

MAIN TEAMS: U.S.: Cuban Stars, New York Cubans
CUBA: Havana MEXICO: Veracruz, Torreón
VENEZUELA: Concordia

POSITIONS: Pitcher, Catcher, First Baseman, Second
Baseman, Third Baseman, Shortstop, Outfielder,
Manager

HEIGHT: 6'3"

WEIGHT: 190 lbs.

BORN: May 25, 1905, Matanzas, Cuba

DIED: May 20, 1971, Cienfuegos, Cuba

Imagine a player who could play every position on the
team, and often did so in one game. Imagine no longer.
Such a player did exist, and he came from Cuba. His name was
Martín Dihigo.

As a center fielder, Dihigo glided into fame as one of the
greatest outfielders of all time. As a second baseman, he is
considered the greatest in Negro League history. Yet it was as
a pitcher that Dihigo gained his fame in Latin America.
Pitching in Mexico one year, he posted a .15 ERA. That is
nearly perfect!

Dihigo could hit, too. In the Negro Leagues, he often won
the home run crown. A Dihigo homer once left the stadium in
Pittsburgh and landed on the roof of a nearby hospital. Another
time, the home run ball just kept on sailing out of the park and
was last seen clearing the weather vane of a nearby house.

In his native Cuba, people called Martín Dihigo "The
Immortal." In the other Latin American countries where he
played, Dihigo was called "El Maestro," The Master. He is the
only player elected to the Baseball Hall of Fame in four
countries — Cuba, Mexico, Venezuela, and the United States.
Some people even say he is the greatest baseball player of
all time.

Martín Dihigo

★ ★ Luis Tiant, Sr. ★ ★

YEARS PLAYED: 1926–1947

MAIN TEAMS: U.S.: Cuban Stars, New York Cubans
CUBA: Almendares, Cienfuegos DOMINICAN REPUBLIC:
Aguilas Cibaeñas MEXICO: Veracruz, Monterrey

POSITION: Pitcher

HEIGHT: 5'11"

WEIGHT: 175 lbs.

BORN: August 27, 1906, Havana, Cuba

DIED: December 12, 1977

Luis Eleuterio Tiant, Sr. may have been the most entertaining Cuban pitcher. "Sir Skinny," as Tiant was called, was a left-handed screwball pitcher who wasn't afraid to throw a spitball. A screwball is a weird curve ball that causes the pitcher's arm to go through a series of painful-looking motions. A spitball is self-explanatory. With these and other crazy pitches, Tiant often led the Cuban League in shutouts. In the 1936–1937 winter season he pitched 12 shutouts, which is still a Cuban record.

Tiant's trademark was his famous pick-off throw to first base. He had a multipronged wind-up that totally confused batters and base stealers. Runners on first base often thought Tiant was starting his wind-up to throw a pitch, so they would wander far from the base. ZAP! the ball would come to first base, and OUT! they would be. In Tiant's most legendary pick-off move, the batter thought the throw was a pitch and swung at a ball that wasn't there. The umpire said to the batter, "If you're dumb enough to swing, it's a strike!"

Tiant's son, Luis Tiant, Jr., went on to become a major league superstar pitcher for the Boston Red Sox. When the younger Tiant retired, he was the all-time Latino strikeout leader in the major leagues. As it turned out, he had a wind-up just as bizarre as his father's. As he lifted his leg, he would turn his back to the catcher, look up at the sky, pivot, and throw. Like father, like son.

Luis Tiant, Sr.

★ ★ Pancho Coímbre ★ ★

YEARS PLAYED: 1926–1946

MAIN TEAMS: U.S.: New York Cubans PUERTO RICO:
   Ponce CUBA: Cuban League MEXICO: Puebla

POSITION: Outfielder

HEIGHT: 5'11"

WEIGHT: 180 lbs.

BORN: January 29, 1909, Coamo, Puerto Rico

DIED: November 4, 1989, Ponce, Puerto Rico

Before there was the world-famous major leaguer Roberto Clemente, there was Francisco "Pancho" Coímbre. He was one of the first baseball heroes from Puerto Rico, and some say the best. Clemente, the first Latin American in the National Baseball Hall of Fame, said that Coímbre was the better player. Coímbre, like so many Latino baseball pioneers, was barred from the major leagues because of his dark skin. But his play in the Negro Leagues and the Puerto Rican League was unbelievably successful.

Although Coímbre was good at everything — fielding, throwing, stealing bases — his specialty was hitting. His lifetime batting average of .337 is the second best in Puerto Rican baseball history. It was nearly impossible to strike Coímbre out. He once went two consecutive years without striking out. And in all of his 1,915 at-bats, Coímbre struck out only 29 times! Here are the batting averages he posted in Puerto Rico for several consecutive seasons during the 1930s and 1940s: .401, .372, .376, .425, .333, .338, .323, .336. In four out of five of his Negro League seasons, Coímbre also put up Hall of Fame batting averages: .330, .353, .436, and .351.

Pancho Coímbre is in the Puerto Rican Baseball Hall of Fame. He is still a hero in Puerto Rico.

Pancho Coímbre

Tetelo Vargas

YEARS PLAYED: 1927–1956

TEAMS: U.S.: New York Cubans DOMINICAN
  REPUBLIC: Escogido, Estrellas Orientales
  PUERTO RICO: Caguas, Guayama, Santurce

POSITION: Center Fielder

HEIGHT: 5'10"

WEIGHT: 160 lbs.

BORN: April 11, 1906, Santo Domingo, Dominican
  Republic

DIED: 1971, Guayama, Puerto Rico

Juan Estéban "Tetelo" Vargas was the first Dominican baseball legend. Little did he know that his homeland would become a major league baseball player factory. These days, half of all Latin American major league players come from the Dominican Republic, a small country on an island in the Caribbean. And many of the Dominican players come from just one town—San Pedro de Macorís. Its specialty: shortstops.

From 1927 until the early 1950s, Tetelo Vargas was one of the best hitters in the Caribbean winter leagues. In 1943, 1946, and 1947, he hit .410, .382, and .362 in the Puerto Rican League. Twice he led that league in hitting and stealing bases. Vargas was *very* fast. A former player once said that Vargas ran as fast as someone who had stolen something other than just a base. In the Negro Leagues, Vargas was twice an All-Star player while playing for the New York Cubans. Once he hit seven straight home runs in seven at-bats. In exhibition games against the New York Yankees, he batted .500!

Even when he was 46 years old, Vargas led the Dominican winter league with a .350 batting average. Tetelo Vargas is in the Puerto Rican Baseball Hall of Fame.

Tetelo Vargas

 Perucho Cepeda

YEARS PLAYED: 1930s–1940s

TEAMS: PUERTO RICO: Guayama

POSITION: Shortstop, First Baseman

HEIGHT: 5'11"

WEIGHT: 200 lbs.

BORN: 1906, San Juan, Puerto Rico

DIED: 1955, Puerto Rico

Pedro Anibal "Perucho" ("The Bull") Cepeda was the greatest Puerto Rican baseball legend *never* to play in the United States. Like Pancho Coímbre, Cepeda was too dark skinned to play in the segregated major leagues. Unlike Coímbre, Cepeda did not play in the Negro Leagues. He did not want any part of the racism that Black baseball players experienced in the United States.

So the proud shortstop stayed in Puerto Rico where he became the Puerto Rican League's first batting champion. That was during the 1938–1939 winter season, and Cepeda hit .365! The next three years he hit .383, .423, and an amazing .464, which is still the highest single season batting average in Puerto Rican baseball history.

Cepeda was called "The Bull" because of his muscular build and his quick temper. He hit balls hard and he hit them far, just like his major league National Hall of Fame son, Orlando Cepeda, "The Baby Bull." Some fans say the father was the better player. We'll never know for sure. But we do know that Perucho Cepeda was a great slugger who is in the Puerto Rican Baseball Hall of Fame.

Perucho Cepeda

★ ★ Bobby Avila ★ ★

YEARS PLAYED: 1941–1959

MAIN TEAMS: U.S.: Cleveland Indians MEXICO: Puebla

POSITION: Infielder

HEIGHT: 5'10"

WEIGHT: 175 lbs.

BORN: April 2, 1924, Veracruz, Mexico

Roberto "Bobby" Francisco Avila González started playing baseball in Mexico in 1941, when he was only 17. He became an overnight star, and had his skin been a little lighter, Avila would have jumped right over to the major leagues in the United States.

In 1949, two years after Jackie Robinson broke the major league "color barrier," Avila did make that jump, joining the Cleveland Indians as the first Mexican player in the major leagues. In his first full major league season with the Indians, Avila hit .301. In his second full season, 1952, he led the American League with 11 triples. A three-time .300-hitter, Avila also made the All-Star team three times. In 1954, he hit .341 and became the first Latino batting champion, beating out the immortal Ted Williams for the crown. And that was with a broken thumb! That year, Avila was voted Player of the Year by *The Sporting News.*

When Avila slid into a base, he sometimes inadvertently kicked the ball from the infielder's glove. That often annoyed the infielder. Other than that, Avila was a perfect gentleman. When he retired in 1959, he returned to his home town of Veracruz and was elected mayor.

Roberto Avila opened the major league door for Mexican baseball players of the future.

Bobby Avila

Minnie Miñoso

YEARS PLAYED: 1945–1973, 1976, 1980

MAIN TEAMS: U.S.: New York Cubans, Chicago White Sox CUBA: Marianao MEXICO: Jalisco, Torreón

POSITION: Outfielder, Third Baseman

HEIGHT: 5'10"

WEIGHT: 175 lbs.

BORN: November 29, 1922, Havana, Cuba

It was May 1, 1951. He stood in the batter's box in Chicago's Comiskey Park, the first Latin American player to wear the Chicago White Sox uniform. It felt as if all Chicago was watching him, waiting to see if he would fail or succeed. In came the first pitch. THWACK! He smashed the ball straight away to dead center field and over the fence. HOME RUN! In his first Chicago at-bat!

That was Saturnino Orestes Arrieta Miñoso Armas.

"Minnie," as he was soon called, brought major league fans a Cuban style of playing baseball that was brand new to them. He seemed to be always running, stealing bases, and making the game exciting. He had style, pizzazz, and blinding speed. He led the league in triples three times, hit over .300 eight times, and led the league in base stealing three times. Eventually, every time Miñoso got on base, Chicago fans would yell, "Go, Minnie, go!" Soon the 1950s Chicago White Sox were nicknamed the Go-Go White Sox, and Miñoso became known as "The Cuban Comet."

During his time with the White Sox, Miñoso fielded more than just balls. Some fans shouted racial taunts at him. Pitchers often knocked him down with their pitches. Instead of getting angry, Miñoso would smile and throw the ball back. He wouldn't let anyone get under his skin.

By the time Miñoso retired, many people considered him the most popular Chicago White Sox player ever.

Minnie Miñoso

Roberto Clemente

YEARS PLAYED: 1952–1972

TEAMS: U.S.: Pittsburgh Pirates PUERTO RICO: Caguas, San Juan, Santurce

POSITION: Outfielder

HEIGHT: 5'11"

WEIGHT: 175 lbs.

BORN: August 18, 1934, Carolina, Puerto Rico

DIED: December 31, 1972, San Juan, Puerto Rico

Roberto Clemente Walker, "The Pride of Puerto Rico," was one of the great all-around baseball players. But Clemente's story is bittersweet. At the peak of his career he died in a plane crash on his way to help earthquake victims in Nicaragua. Most people, not just baseball fans, knew who Clemente was, and most were shocked and saddened by his sudden death.

As it turned out, Clemente died just after reaching a career peak few baseball players ever reach: 3,000 hits. He got every one of these hits while playing with the Pittsburgh Pirates. He won 12 Gold Glove Awards, appeared in 14 All-Star games, and had a .317 lifetime batting average. Upon his death, Clemente was quickly elected to the National Baseball Hall of Fame, its first Latin American member. No one before or since has ever been elected so fast.

The spectacular dives and leaps Clemente made in the field were unlike anything most fans in the United States had ever seen. Clemente's enthusiasm, pride, and emotion when he played were sometimes misunderstood by players, managers, fans, and the press, and reporters often called him a showoff and a hothead. This upset Clemente, and he was not afraid to speak out against the racism he experienced.

No one has been more of a role model for young Latin American players than Clemente. He stood up for himself while he showed the world exactly how dazzling a Latino baseball player could be.

Roberto Clemente

Luis Aparicio

YEARS PLAYED: 1953–1973

MAIN TEAMS: U.S.: Chicago White Sox, Baltimore Orioles VENEZUELA: Guaira

POSITION: Shortstop

HEIGHT: 5'8"

WEIGHT: 162 lbs.

BORN: April 29, 1934, Maracaibo, Venezuela

People have been playing baseball in Venezuela for a long time, and fair-skinned Venezuelans were playing in the major leagues as early as 1939. But the first Venezuelan superstar did not arrive on the major league scene until 1956. As soon as Luis Aparicio, Jr. started playing, fans were checking their scorecards and asking, "Who is this guy?"

From his first season with the Chicago White Sox in 1956, Aparicio was tearing up the base paths. That year he was elected Rookie of the Year. From there, Aparicio went on to become the undisputed base-stealing champion, leading the American League in stolen bases from 1956 through 1964— nine years straight!

Amazingly, stealing bases was not Aparicio's main claim to fame. He was one of the greatest shortstops of all time, maybe even *the* greatest. He still holds many of the major league records for shortstops, including:

★ most career double plays
★ most career games
★ most career assists
★ most career putouts in the American League

Being light skinned and fluent in English, Aparicio did not encounter the racism other Latin American players often faced. Being a gentleman and an incredible player, Aparicio had about as smooth a major league career as any Latino. He was named an All-Star player eight times and slid right into the National Baseball Hall of Fame.

Luis Aparicio

Juan Marichal

YEARS PLAYED: 1960–1975

MAIN TEAMS: U.S.: San Francisco Giants

DOMINICAN REPUBLIC: Escogido

POSITION: Pitcher

HEIGHT: 6'0"

WEIGHT: 185 lbs.

BORN: October 20, 1937, Laguna Verde, Dominican Republic

Baseball is a sport, but—and this is very important—baseball is also entertainment. Some baseball players are just more entertaining than others. They are more fun to watch. One such player was a Dominican pitcher named Juan Antonio Marichal.

"The Dominican Dandy," as Marichal was called by non-Latinos, was a right-handed pitching wizard with a wind-up that turned people's heads and made them want to dance. It wasn't just that he kicked his left leg high when getting ready to throw a ball, he also kicked it straight out. It was his trademark, a signature, a way of saying, "Just try to hit *this* ball!"

Marichal backed up his style with marvelous playing. He was named to 10 All-Star teams. When he retired, he had the second lowest ERA in National League history: 2.89, with 2,303 strikeouts and a 243–142 win-loss record. Marichal's winning percentage was .631, the sixth best in major league history among pitchers winning 200 games or more.

Juan Marichal was the first Latin American pitcher elected to the National Baseball Hall of Fame. He opened the major league door to a new, exciting style of pitching. Baseball in the United States hasn't been the same since.

Juan Marichal

Felipe Alou

YEARS PLAYED: 1958–1974, 1992–2001

MAIN TEAMS: U.S.: San Francisco Giants,
   Milwaukee/Atlanta Braves, Montreal Expos
   DOMINICAN REPUBLIC: Escogido

POSITION: Outfielder, Manager

HEIGHT: 6'1"

WEIGHT: 195 lbs.

BORN: May 12, 1935, Haina, Dominican Republic

Felipe Rojas Alou was the first Dominican to become a full-time player in the major leagues. He was also the first Dominican manager in the majors, and in 1994, Alou was the first Latino to win the Manager of the Year award.

As a young player, Alou sparkled on the San Francisco Giants. His two brothers, Matty and Jesús, also played with the Giants. For one game in 1963, all three brothers played the Giants outfield together. All three were good players, but Felipe was a three-time All-Star player and a two-time National League leader in hits. He had three seasons in which he hit over .300 and had a respectable .287 lifetime batting average.

From the beginning of his baseball career in the United States, Alou was a spokesperson for Latin American ball players. He spoke out against racist attitudes toward himself and other Latinos like Roberto Clemente and Juan Marichal. He fought for a Latin American representative in the Baseball Commissioner's office, someone who would understand Spanish and the different cultures of Latin America. But it was becoming Manager of the major league Montreal Expos in 1992, and leading them to the best record in baseball during 1994, that is Alou's greatest accomplishment so far. Success as a major league manager was one of the last frontiers for Latin American ball players, and Felipe Alou was its heroic pioneer.

Felipe Alou

The Players at a Glance

 José Méndez
- ★ Called the greatest pitcher of his era
- ◆ .747 lifetime winning percentage

 Dolf Luque
- ★ First Latin American star in the major leagues
- ◆ Won 27 games in one year, 1923

 Cristóbal Torriente
- ★ Called the "Cuban Babe Ruth"
- ◆ .351 lifetime batting average in Cuba; .327 in the United States

 Martín Dihigo
- ★ Most versatile baseball player ever
- ◆ Elected to the Baseball Hall of Fame in Cuba, Mexico, Venezuela, and the United States

 Luis Tiant, Sr.
- ★ Legendary Cuban screwball pitcher
- ◆ Famous for his pick-off throw to first base

 Pancho Coímbre
- ★ First great Puerto Rican baseball legend
- ◆ .337 lifetime batting average

 Tetelo Vargas
- ★ First Dominican baseball legend, noted for his speed
- ◆ Batted .500 in exhibition games against the New York Yankees

 Perucho Cepeda
- ★ Greatest Puerto Rican baseball legend *never* to play in the U.S.
- ◆ Puerto Rican League's first batting champion

 Bobby Avila
- ★ First Mexican star in the major leagues
- ◆ Voted 1954 Player of the Year by *The Sporting News*

 Minnie Miñoso
- ★ Most popular Chicago White Sox player of the 1950s
- ◆ Called "The Cuban Comet" for his base-running speed

 Roberto Clemente
- ★ Most famous Latin American baseball legend
- ◆ Played in 14 All-Star games; won 12 Gold Gloves; .317 lifetime batting average

 Luis Aparicio
- ★ First Venezuelan star in the major leagues
- ◆ Holds many major league records for shortstops

 Juan Marichal
- ★ One of the first Dominican stars in the major leagues
- ◆ 2.89 lifetime ERA, second best in National League history

 Felipe Alou
- ★ Played in three All-Star games
- ◆ First Latin American Manager of the Year